WOMEN WINNING THE RIGHT TO VOTE

IN UNITED STATES HISTORY

★ IN ★
UNITED STATES
★ HISTORY ★

★ CAROL RUST NASH ★

Enslow Publishers, Inc.
40 Industrial Road
Box 398
Berkeley Heights, NJ 07922
USA

http://www.enslow.com

This book is dedicated to my sister, Jo Ann Rust,
whose life is an example of independence and liberation.

Originally published as *The Fight for Women's Right to Vote in American History* in 1998.

Library of Congress Cataloging-in-Publication Data

Nash, Carol Rust.
    Women winning the right to vote in united states history / Carol Rust Nash.
        pages cm. — (In United States History)
        Rev. ed. of: Fight for women's right to vote in American history, c1998.
        Includes bibliographical references and index.
        ISBN 978-0-7660-6073-9
        1. Women—Suffrage—United States—History—Juvenile literature.
        2. Women's rights—United States—History—Juvenile literature. [1. Women—
    Suffrage. 2. Women's rights—History.] I. Nash, Carol Rust. Fight for women's
    right to vote in American history. II. Title.
    JK1898.N38 2014
    324.6'230973—dc23
                                                            2013047134

Future Editions:
Paperback ISBN: 978-0-7660-6074-6
EPUB ISBN: 978-0-7660-6075-3
Single-User PDF ISBN: 978-0-7660-6076-0
Multi-User PDF ISBN: 978-0-7660-6077-7

Printed in the United States of America
072014 HF Group, North Manchester, IN
10 9 8 7 6 5 4 3 2

To Our Readers: We have done our best to make sure all Internet addresses in this book were active and appropriate when we went to press. However, the author and the publisher have no control over and assume no liability for the material available on those Internet sites or on other Web sites they may link to. Any comments can be sent by e-mail to comments@enslow.com or to the address on the back cover.

Illustration Credits: Enslow Publishers, Inc., p. 54; Library of Congress, p. 1;

Cover Illustrations: Library of Congress.

Cover Description: Two women suffragists, Mrs. Stanley McCormick and Mrs. Charles Parker, holding a banner between them reading "National Woman Suffrage Association." April 22, 1913. The National Woman Suffrage Association (NWSA) was founded in 1869. It became one of the two leading organizations fighting for women's suffrage.

☆ CONTENTS ☆

Acknowledgments

Special thanks go to Deborah McKown,
my friend and copy editor, for suggestions and support.

Chapter 1

CALL TO ACTION

Remember the Ladies, and be more generous and favourable to them than your ancestors. Do not put such unlimited power into the hands of the Husbands. . . . If perticuliar care and attention is not paid to the Laidies [sic] we are determined to foment a Rebellion.[1]

—Abigail Adams

Battle for Equality

The rebellion began as Abigail Adams predicted in the letter above. The battle for women's right to vote officially began at the Seneca Falls Women's Rights Convention in 1848—over seventy years after Adams's 1776 letter to her husband—and continued for seventy-two years before victory was achieved. It would become one of the longest-lasting reform movements in American history.[2]

The Battle's Philosopher

Elizabeth Cady was born into a prominent New York family in 1815. She received the best education available to women at that time, attending Emma Willard's Troy Seminary. But she was not happy about it. She was furious that she could not attend Union College, which was for boys only.[3] Though Troy offered a serious education, it did not emphasize the classics the way boys-only schools did.

Unlike many other women who believed that government and politics were activities suitable for men only, Cady read the law in her father's office after her graduation. She became a student of legal and constitutional history.

Cady met Henry B. Stanton, a brilliant abolitionist organizer, through her activities in the abolition movement, an organized attempt to end slavery in the United States. Stanton was in the process of forming a new antislavery party, the Liberty Party. Both Cady and Stanton believed that political organization was necessary for reform.[4]

After a brief engagement, they were married in 1840, between the founding convention of the Liberty Party and a meeting of the American Anti-Slavery Society. It was at this meeting that the Anti-Slavery Society's membership split over the question of women's rights. Some thought women should be voting members; others disagreed.

The first stop on the Stantons' honeymoon was the home of leaders of the antislavery movement: Angelina Grimké Weld, Theodore Weld, and Sarah Grimké. From there, Elizabeth Cady Stanton—who kept her birth name as well as her husband's name after the marriage, which was an unusual practice at that time—and her new husband set out for the World's Anti-Slavery Convention in London.

Due to the recent split in the United States abolition movement over the role of women, a bitter controversy developed at the convention over women's rights in general. The women delegates from the United States were not allowed into the convention.

Lucretia Mott, an abolitionist and feminist, was one of the delegates refused admittance. A Quaker housewife, Mott had persuaded her husband to give up a business that was dependent on African-American slaves, and she exposed ministers who were slaveholders. She had indeed done her part to abolish slavery, so it was unfair that she was not allowed in the convention. She decided that in order for women to have a voice in society, they first needed the vote.

Elizabeth Cady Stanton was also banned from the convention. She and Mott spent a great deal of time together in London and began a correspondence when they returned to the United States.

Battle Lines

In 1848, Stanton organized the first women's rights convention. She was aided by Mott and her sister, Martha Wright, as well as another Quaker woman, Mary Ann McClintock. Stanton suggested adapting the Declaration of Independence as a statement of women's rights. She put together a list of complaints designed to prove that history was a record of men's injustices toward women. This document, the first public protest in the United States against women's political, economic, and social inferiority, was called the Declaration of Sentiments.

Men made the laws that gave them control over women's wages and property, that gave husbands authority over their wives, and that deprived women of their children in divorce. Stanton believed that for these conditions to change, women had to take a role in society in addition to wife and mother. They needed political equality. They needed the vote.[5]

When the Declaration of Sentiments was adopted at Seneca Falls, the women's rights movement, which would focus on women's right to vote, was launched. In 1850, two years after the Seneca Falls convention, another convention was held in Akron, Ohio, to put pressure on the state constitutional convention to address the issue of women's political equality. Later that year, a meeting in Worcester, Massachusetts, attracted feminists from eight states. They set up a coordinating committee, a plan for women's right-to-vote (suffrage) campaigns in their states, and committees to report on the educational, industrial, legal, and social status of women. Women organized a convention in Indiana in 1851 and in Pennsylvania in 1852.[6]

Because of her duties as a mother of young children and the demands of running a household, Stanton was unable to attend most of these early conventions. She sent letters of support to them and began planning a book on women's history. She also wrote articles for the *New-York Tribune*.

Amelia Bloomer, also of Seneca Falls, started publishing a monthly women's temperance newspaper called *The Lily*. (*Temperance* means abstinence from alcoholic beverages. The temperance movement advocated making it illegal to sell or possess liquor.) Stanton saw *The Lily* as a way to spread information about women's rights and sold Bloomer on the idea. *The Lily* became the only publication in the country to spread accurate news about the women's rights movement.[7]

Bloomer was also instrumental in changing the style of women's clothing. Women wore corsets so constricting that they cut the amount of air that could be taken into the lungs, which often caused women to faint. Over their corsets, they wore yards of hot, heavy fabric and layers of petticoats that also restricted movement.

Elizabeth Smith Miller, Stanton's cousin and an advocate for dress reform, proposed the Turkish trouser, a full-cut pantaloon worn under a short skirt to reduce the weight and allow more natural movement. Bloomer promoted the new style in her newspaper, and the pantaloons came to be called bloomers.

Bloomers were originally adopted by women for outdoor work. Bloomer and Miller wore them in public for the first time in Seneca Falls in 1851. The costume never really caught on, in part, because it was considered radical—the new, militant women's rights fashion.

The Battle's First General

Susan Brownell Anthony was born in 1820 in a small town in western Massachusetts, the second child of Daniel and Lucy Anthony. Her father was a Quaker, and her mother was loving and committed. Her family, with eight children altogether, was filled with devotion and love.

When Susan was eleven, she asked her father to promote one of the women workers at his mill to overseer. Susan had worked at the mill on occasion and had observed that the woman knew more about weaving than the male overseer. Although progressive, her father said, "It would never do to have a woman overseer in the mill."[8]

Susan's father organized home schools for the families who worked in his factory, but he sent his own children to the district school. One day, Susan came home upset. Her teacher—a man—had refused to teach her long division. Susan believed it was because she was a girl. Quakers believed that girls should receive the same education as boys, and Mr. Anthony was not happy with this news. He pulled his children out of the district school and organized a home school for them. He also created an evening school for his employees.[9]

At first he taught the classes himself, but later he hired a full-time teacher, Mary Perkins, to instruct the children and the employees.

Independent and educated, Perkins represented a new image of womanhood to Susan. However, when she was fourteen, her father sent her to attend Deborah Moulson's Female Seminary, a Quaker boarding school in Hamilton, Pennsylvania. For the first few years, she was intensely homesick, but she taught herself to funnel those powerful feelings into her schoolwork.

In May 1839, at age nineteen, Susan Anthony took a teaching job in New Rochelle, New York. She became an assistant teacher at Eunice Kenyon's Quaker boarding school. Teaching was one of the few professions open to women in the 1840s. It allowed them their own identities and economic independence. Teaching was considered acceptable work for women because it was believed that teaching was much like mothering.

Anthony was twenty-six when she was offered the post of headmistress for the women's department of the Canajoharie Academy in Canajoharie, New York. But after a few years in this position, she became dissatisfied. Teaching made her weary and no longer challenged her. She began to wonder what else she could do with her life.[10]

Taking the antislavery position in arguments with her uncle and cousins, who opposed change, energized her, and the temperance movement caught her attention.[11] She became a member of the Canajoharie Daughters of Temperance. Through her organizing efforts and speeches, she became aware of the larger world and began to question social injustice. She reflected on her mother's life, and soon began to reflect on women's lives in general.

In 1849, Anthony resigned her teaching post and returned home to help run the family farm in Rochester, New York. There, she often helped runaway slaves coming through Rochester on the Underground Railroad. The city was their last stop before reaching Canada and their freedom. Anthony decided that it was time to further educate herself about the antislavery movement.

In May 1851, Anthony went to Syracuse for a series of antislavery meetings. Though not involved in women's rights issues at the time, Anthony wanted to meet the radical and controversial Elizabeth Cady Stanton. She was disappointed when Stanton did not attend the meetings.

Stanton and Anthony Meet

Anthony met Amelia Bloomer in Syracuse to hear abolitionist speakers at the antislavery meetings. After the meetings, Bloomer invited Anthony to her home in Seneca Falls, which was the next stop on the speakers' lecture tour. Anthony accepted the invitation, hoping she might meet Stanton there.

Anthony and Stanton did meet after the antislavery lectures, but Stanton was preoccupied, worrying about what mischief her boys were up to at home. The two women exchanged pleasantries and Stanton left abruptly. Anthony stood on the street corner, disappointed again.[12]

Their second meeting was initiated by Stanton, who invited Anthony to stay at her home in Seneca Falls for several days. There, she would meet avid abolitionist and suffragist Lucy Stone and Horace Greeley, a journalist and political leader. They were coming to discuss a plan for a coeducational college.

Stone, fiercely independent, had worked her way through college. Fighting for suffrage and believing in the revolutionary cry of "No taxation without representation," she refused to pay taxes on her property and allowed it to be sold for payment. Because she could not vote to elect her representatives, she said that she was taxed without representation.

Stone had kept her birth name when she married Henry Blackwell rather than take his, a practice that was highly unusual during the mid-1800s. Women who followed her lead by keeping their names when they married were referred to as Stoneites.[13]

Stone was an eloquent speaker and one of the most important of the early suffragists. Her husband was also an avid proponent of women's voting rights. When they married, they issued a joint statement saying they were to be equals in all things. Blackwell renounced the rights over his wife that the law granted him as husband.

The plan for a coeducational college did not develop when Anthony met Stone and Greeley, but a deep affection between Anthony and Stanton did. They remained close for fifty years.

Though they were good friends, their lives were very different. Anthony was finding her place in the public world. Stanton was enclosing herself in her domestic world, having babies and raising a family. Anthony's self-discipline offset Stanton's flamboyance, openness, and enthusiasm. Anthony liked Stanton's bold ideas. Stanton liked Anthony's independence of mind and spirit.[14]

Anthony visited Seneca Falls whenever she could. She brought the world of reform and her craving for action to Stanton.

Their intellectual and emotional compatibility charged both women. Their differences made their work and their partnership more effective. Over the years, Stanton became known as the "philosopher," and Anthony was called the "general" of the suffrage movement. Stanton described their relationship well when she said:

> In writing we did better work together than either could alone. While she is slow and analytical in composition, I am rapid and synthetic. I am the better writer, she the better critic. She supplied the facts and statistics, I the philosophy and rhetoric, and together we have made arguments that have stood unshaken by the storms of thirty long years; arguments that no man has answered.[15]

Chapter 2

A NATION AT WAR

It is doubtful if any man, even among suffrage men, ever realized what the suffrage struggle came to mean to women before the end was allowed in America. . . . It leaves its mark on one, such a struggle.[1]

—Carrie Chapman Catt and Nettie Rogers Shuler

Secession

The second half of the nineteenth century—the years that encompassed the bulk of the women's rights movement—was a turbulent period in U.S. history. The national debate over slavery and states' rights dominated public attention as it grew increasingly divisive. It led eleven Southern states to secede (withdraw) from the Union. In 1860 and 1861, those states formed the Confederate States of America. The Civil War followed shortly thereafter.

The women's suffrage movement was woven throughout this turmoil, intertwined with the struggle against slavery. Early leaders of the women's rights movement fought two battles on the front lines of the war against slavery—the issue of slavery itself and the right to speak publicly.

The pressures silencing women came not only from society, but from fellow activists as well. Though many abolitionists saw the battle as one of human rights, which included rights for women, others feared that linking women's rights to abolition might defeat abolition, which was the primary goal at the time. Some simply did not want women to speak from the abolitionist platforms because they did not want to make their task of persuading people to oppose slavery any more difficult.[2]

Women's Movement Begins

It was during the antislavery crusade that the organized women's rights movement began in the United States. In 1838, ten years prior to the Seneca Falls convention, Angelina Grimké said, "The discussion of the rights of the slave has opened the way for the discussion of *other* rights."[3]

The temperance movement also gave the women's rights movement a push. Because of her dislike for the men who were leading the temperance movement, Susan B. Anthony talked Elizabeth Cady Stanton into organizing the Woman's New York State Temperance Society. Five hundred women attended the society's first meeting, held in April 1852. Stanton was named president and Anthony secretary.

Stanton proposed a women's rights program for the new organization. She called for women's suffrage and for divorce laws that would permit women to divorce drunken husbands.

These ideas proved to be too radical for many temperance women. At the first-anniversary meeting of the society, Stanton and Anthony were challenged by conservative temperance women and men. First, the rule against men voting in the society was overturned, then Stanton was removed as president. The issues of divorce and women's suffrage were dropped, and the organization focused on temperance only. Anthony was reelected but withdrew to show solidarity with Stanton.

Anthony and Stanton Speak Out

Anthony never shied away from speaking up or making her point. At the 1853 state convention of schoolteachers, female teachers were allowed to attend but not to speak.

Anthony sat silently as a long discussion took place about why the profession was not as respected as medicine, law, or the ministry. When she could stand it no longer, she stood up and shouted, "Mr. President!"[4] Asked what she wanted, she said that she wished to speak about the issue.

After the convention leadership debated and voted, they agreed to let her speak. She explained to them that the cause of the disrespect was that society had said that women were incompetent to be doctors, lawyers, or ministers. Since they, male teachers, had chosen a profession that allowed women within its ranks, they must have had "no more brains than a woman."[5] She went on to explain that teaching was less lucrative than other professions because men had to compete with the cheap labor of women. She argued that if the salaries of female teachers—who were "engaged in the noble work of educating our future Presidents, Senators, and Congressmen"—were increased, the profession would become both more lucrative and well-respected.[6] Thus Anthony introduced the revolutionary idea of equal pay for equal work.

In 1857 Anthony became a paid organizer for the American Anti-Slavery Society. For four years, she traveled extensively for the cause and, at the same time, directed women's rights campaigns in New York.

Stanton also joined the antislavery society that year. She was asked to address a meeting of the society in 1860. Her speech was about black slaves, white women, and the link between abolition and women's rights. She was criticized by some in the society for putting too much emphasis on women's rights.[7]

Beginnings of Civil War

In an attempt to inspire a slave rebellion, abolitionist John Brown built a private army and raided a United States arsenal at Harpers Ferry, Virginia, in October 1859. The pro-slavery forces saw the raid as proof that abolitionists were conspiring with African Americans to mount a rebellion. Brown was captured, charged with treason, and hanged.

Stanton had believed in Brown's cause. After the failure of the raid, Stanton's respect for Brown moved her to protest slavery publicly.[8] In early 1861, Stanton joined Anthony in her first traveling campaign, which included a series of antislavery meetings in western New York. They were harassed and attacked physically as they demanded, in city after city, that the newly elected Republican president, Abraham Lincoln, make a commitment to the abolition of slavery.[9] Though the North was generally antislavery, many Northerners held abolitionists responsible for the secession of the South and the war that was soon to come.

On April 12, 1861, the secessionist government of South Carolina attacked federal forces at Fort Sumter in Charleston Harbor. Virginia, Arkansas, Tennessee, and North Carolina joined the Confederacy. The Civil War had begun.

War Years

The war between the states dominated political life. Women's rights issues were put on hold until the issue of slavery was resolved. Stanton and Anthony headed the National Woman's Loyal League, which called for support of the Union and rallied thousands of women to political action in defense of the war effort. The Radicals, allies of the abolitionists in the Republican Party, became sympathetic to women's rights advocates because of the league's pro-war activities.[10]

Feminists who had previously shied away from political organizations and institutions had their eyes opened to the realities of political power by the wartime campaign for African-American rights. Before the war, many had seen the right to vote as the central principle of the many needed changes. The war to free the slaves showed them the necessity of participation in the political process to achieve their goal.[11]

After the War

The end of the Civil War in April 1865 opened a difficult period of national healing, debate, and decision making. Reconstruction, the process of bringing back the states that had seceded, lasted until 1877. During this period, the issue that dominated politics was black suffrage—the legal status of former slaves hinged on their winning the right to vote.

The Radicals believed that freedmen had the same "natural right" or "equal right" to life, liberty, and property as white men. To protect those rights, they needed political power—the vote.[12] Feminists were counting on the equal rights ideology to add the rights of women to the Reconstruction debate.

In 1866, Stanton and Anthony reorganized the women's rights movement to tie it in more closely with the drive for black suffrage. They formed the American Equal Rights Association (AERA) to combine the two demands for suffrage into one campaign: the right to vote for all adults.

The association's first order of business was to fight the wording of the proposed Fourteenth Amendment to the Constitution. The amendment defined citizenship as the rights and privileges a United States citizen enjoys. It specifically stated that no state could deny its citizens the rights and privileges they already had as citizens of the United States. It was designed to protect the rights of the recently freed African Americans. However, it excluded women by specifying that representation in Congress would only be based on the population of male citizens in the state.

The AERA petitioned Congress, but Radicals refused to introduce the AERA's petition in Congress, fearing a link with women's suffrage would weaken the demand for African-American suffrage. The amendment was passed by Congress in June 1866 and was ratified by the states in 1868. It was the first time the word *male* had appeared in the Constitution.

Before the amendment took effect, abolitionists and Radicals urged feminists to wait until the freedmen's rights were secure before pushing forward for their own.[13] The Radicals, who were within the Republican Party, were promising help later on. The Republicans, however, called it the "Negro's hour," making it clear that women's suffrage would have to wait and giving no promise of support.[14]

The AERA faced a dilemma. To demand women's suffrage at the expense of African Americans was a betrayal of abolitionism. To support African-American rights over women's rights was an unreasonable sacrifice.

The issue caused a split among feminist groups. One group accepted the priority of African-American suffrage. Under the leadership of Lucy Stone, it also accepted the Radicals' promises that they would work for women's suffrage as soon as the right to vote for African-American men was secure.

Stanton and Anthony could not accept the terms of delay. They pushed ahead to fight for women's suffrage without any expectation of Republican support and without the aid of Radicals or abolitionists. The movement entered uncharted waters. It now had its primary support from women alone.

Anthony and Stanton argued bitterly for women's suffrage and, despite their abolitionist backgrounds, often used racist tactics. They abandoned their black sisters and argued that because white women were educated and virtuous, they deserved the vote more than ex-slaves. They thought it would be better to defeat the Fourteenth Amendment than to have it recognize men only. Showing a militant feminist spirit, they distanced themselves from abolitionists. They were committed to an independent organization of women.

In 1868 they started *The Revolution*, a boldly radical feminist newspaper. Its motto was "Men, their rights, and nothing more; women, their rights, and nothing less."[15]

After Congress passed the Fifteenth Amendment in 1869, which ensured the voting rights of African-American men, there was discussion in Congress of a possible Sixteenth Amendment for women's suffrage. The two factions of the women's rights movement met again. In spring 1869, the divided AERA met, only to discover the differences were still too great. Stone and her allies could not forgive Stanton and Anthony for their racial slurs and for opposing the Fourteenth and Fifteenth Amendments.[16] In addition, the two factions differed on their preferred method for winning suffrage. Stone's group emphasized a state-by-state strategy over a federal amendment. They thought the only way to obtain a federal women's suffrage amendment was to win one state at a time. They reasoned that when a majority of states had passed state amendments allowing women to vote, a federal amendment would follow. Stanton and Anthony still believed the best method was to get the vote for all women with just one national amendment.

Two separate organizations were established. Stanton and Anthony founded the National Woman Suffrage Association (NWSA) in May 1869. Stone started the American Woman Suffrage Association (AWSA).

The separation would last for more than two decades, spreading thin the women's suffrage movement's energies, resources, and supporters.

ONE WOMAN VOTES

It [the lack of women's suffrage] is not chiefly because good men fear the influence of bad politics on good women, but because bad men fear the influence of good women on bad politics.[1]

—Carrie Chapman Catt

Paving the Way

After it became clear that women's suffrage would not be part of the Fourteenth or Fifteenth Amendments to the Constitution, a new approach was proposed by Victoria Woodhull.

Woodhull was a forceful advocate of equality between men and women. Her philosophy was similar to that of Elizabeth Cady Stanton's: She wanted the vote for the freedom it would give women. Woodhull was a leader of the United States wing of the International Workingmen's Association, a socialist group that Karl Marx had formed in London in 1864. She was also the first woman to run for president of the United States. She ran on the People's Party platform in 1872, but her unsuccessful campaign did little more than organize the party.

Woodhull devised a much simpler plan for achieving women's suffrage than a constitutional amendment. She argued that a congressional act or judicial decision would be sufficient to give women the vote because the right was already granted to them by the Constitution.

Her argument stated: The Fourteenth and Fifteenth amendments said that all people born or naturalized in the United States were national citizens; the rights of all citizens were protected by the Constitution; therefore, assuming that all women were people and suffrage was a right of citizenship, women were already entitled to vote.

In January 1871, Woodhull presented her proposal to the Judiciary Committee of the House of Representatives. It was the first time a woman had appeared before Congress on behalf of women's suffrage.

One month after the hearing, committee chairman John A. Bingham issued a report rejecting Woodhull's proposal. The committee denied that the Fourteenth and Fifteenth amendments granted voting rights to women.

However, Woodhull's argument was adopted by the National Woman Suffrage Association (NWSA). Two years before Woodhull's attempt, in 1869, Virginia Minor had made a similar proposal to the association. At that time, suffragists believed that their road to the polls should be the same one African-American men had taken, and they did not give the proposal serious consideration.[2] By 1871, their attitude had changed.

Based on the constitutional argument, the NWSA encouraged women "to go to the polls, submit their ballots, and dare election officials to refuse them."[3] This would put the burden on men to refuse the votes of women and to explain why they were refusing fellow citizens the right to vote. Hundreds of women all over the country tried to vote in the elections of 1871 and 1872.

Registering and Voting

Susan B. Anthony was determined to vote. Not only was she eager to test the constitutional waters, but Republicans had offered feminists a small plank in the party's platform, guaranteeing "respectful consideration" regarding women's demands of "additional rights."[4] Both Stanton and Anthony had worked for the party, and Anthony wanted to cast her vote of support.

Anthony and her three sisters, along with about fifty other women in Rochester, marched off to register to vote in the 1872 election. E. T. Marsh, the election inspector, was a neighbor of Anthony's and young enough to be her son. He said that Anthony "DEMANDED that we register them as voters."[5]

Marsh and the other male election inspectors told Anthony and her companions that they could not be registered because they were women. Anthony read them the Fourteenth Amendment to the United States Constitution and an article from the New York State Constitution. She pointed out that neither document contained any qualifications for voting based on sex. The men held firm.

"If you still refuse us our rights as citizens, I will bring charges against you in Criminal Court and I will sue each of you personally for large, exemplary damages! I know I can win," Anthony said.[6]

The inspectors were intimidated. They discussed the problem and agreed to get legal counsel before making a decision. A prominent lawyer and strong supporter of women's right to vote suggested that the inspectors have the women take all the oaths of registry because "that would put the entire [burden] of the affair on them."[7] Women were registered to vote.

Early on the morning of November 5, 1872, Anthony and fourteen other women in her Rochester ward voted. Later that day, the press demanded that anyone who allowed women to vote be arrested. The intimidation was successful, and many of the women who had been allowed to register were not allowed to vote.

The Arrest

On November 18, more than three weeks after Anthony had cast her first vote, a deputy United States marshal came to her home and informed her, "The commissioner wishes to arrest you."[8] He explained that the arrest was for illegal voting.

The marshal produced the warrant for her arrest, to which Anthony replied that she was not properly dressed for court. He waited in the parlor while she changed. She came down the stairs, stood before him, and held up her wrists to be handcuffed. He insisted that cuffs were not necessary and took her away without them.

Anthony joined the inspectors who had registered her and the fourteen other women from her ward who had voted.

A hearing was set for December 23, and each party was released on five-hundred-dollars bail. Anthony was the only one to refuse bail.

Her lawyer applied for a writ of habeas corpus, arguing that she had exercised a right and had not committed a crime. (Habeas corpus is a legal petition filed to seek prompt release of someone in custody. It places the burden of proof on those detaining the person to justify the arrest.) Anthony was released, pending a decision on the writ.

A United States district judge denied the writ after listening to arguments on January 21, 1873, and increased her bail to one thousand dollars. Anthony again refused to pay bail and stated that she would rather go to jail than cooperate. Despite her objections, her lawyer, Henry Selden, put up the bail.

With the payment of bail, Anthony lost her chance to take her case to the United States Supreme Court by writ of habeas corpus, which had been her plan. Her lawyer admitted that he had known what would happen because of his action, but said, "I could not see a lady I respected put in jail."[9]

Anthony considered Selden a good lawyer and a kind person, but she was angry that her plans had been ruined by a man's attempt to protect her.[10]

Anthony voted again in a local election on March 4 while awaiting trial. This time she was the only woman to vote. The others had been frightened away by the threat of fines or imprisonment. Anthony visited every district of Monroe County—where she was to be tried—and spoke about the legal and constitutional issues involved in her case. The court decided that the trial should be moved to another county because her public speaking had influenced potential jurors.

On May 23 the case was moved out of Monroe County to Canandaigua in Ontario County. The trial was rescheduled for June 17. Anthony immediately launched another speaking campaign, this one in Ontario County. She made her last speech the night before her trial began.

The Trial

Henry Selden argued for three hours in Anthony's defense before United States Associate Justice Ward Hunt. Because Anthony was a woman, she was not allowed to speak in her own defense.

Following Selden, the district attorney responded. After the arguments from both sides were presented, Justice Hunt took a piece of paper from his pocket and read his opinion, taking the decision out of the jury's hands.

Hunt said that the Fourteenth Amendment did not cover Anthony's right to vote. The amendment was a protection of citizens' rights as they existed, which did not include women's right to vote.

Hunt believed Anthony had influenced the jury with her public speaking, so he had written his opinion before hearing the arguments. Though this was a criminal case that was constitutionally protected by the right to trial by jury, Hunt directed the jury to find Anthony guilty.

Selden protested and demanded that the jury be polled. Without hearing the verdict from the jurors, Hunt discharged them.

Anthony attempted to explain why the verdict was unjust. The judge stopped her and told her the court could not allow her to go on.

She continued anyway, explaining that she had not been tried by a jury of her peers and, therefore, had just cause for protest. Claiming that she failed to get justice, Anthony said, "I ask not leniency at your hands—but rather the full rigors of the law."[11] However, she continued,

> May it please your honor, I shall never pay a dollar of your unjust penalty. . . . And I shall earnestly and persistently continue to urge all women to the practical recognition of the old revolutionary maxim, that "Resistance to tyranny is obedience to God."[12]

Anthony refused to pay the fine. Hunt, however, refused to have her imprisoned until the fine was paid. It was a deliberate move on his part. If he had imprisoned her, she could have taken her case to the United States Supreme Court through a writ of habeas corpus. By not allowing her to be jailed, he prevented her from proceeding with her case.

The Supreme Court Decision

Even without Anthony, the argument that the Fourteenth and Fifteenth Amendments gave women the right to vote finally reached the highest court in the land in 1875. In the case of *Minor* v. *Happersett*, Francis Minor filed a suit in Missouri on behalf of his wife, Virginia Minor.[13] (Because she was a woman, Virginia could not bring suit in her own name.) Minor argued that the Constitution already granted women the right to vote.

The Supreme Court rejected the argument and ruled that suffrage was not a right of national citizenship, but a privilege granted by each individual state.

Because the argument based on the wording of the Fourteenth Amendment had failed, suffragists picked up the battle for a new amendment to guarantee women the right to vote. Almost another half century of struggle lay ahead.

4 Chapter

MOVEMENT WEST

*D*isfranchisement is the prison of women's power and spirit.[1]

—Katharine Fisher,
Massachusetts National Woman's Party leader

The first state to give women complete voting privileges was Wyoming. In 1869, the territorial government of Wyoming decreed political equality. This gave women the right not only to vote, but to hold political office and serve on juries. The Wyoming law establishing political equality of the sexes was the first of its kind in the United States. When Wyoming entered the Union in 1890, it became the first state with full suffrage for women.

In 1896, women in Idaho also won the vote. Women were making an impact in the West.

Suffrage in Utah

The Utah territorial legislature voted to give women suffrage in 1870. The victory was clouded by a complex political struggle, however. Mormons—members of the Church of Jesus Christ of Latter-day Saints—made up the majority of the population of the Utah Territory. The Mormons also dominated Utah politics, which caused concern in the federal government. If one church were so strong, how could separation of religion and politics be assured?

In 1887, Congress passed the Edmunds-Tucker Act in an effort to stop Mormon control of Utah's government. It also took away the right of women to vote.

Though Mormon and non-Mormon women did not see eye to eye on the religious issues in Utah, being stripped of the right to vote brought them together in the national suffrage movement. In 1896, after a nine-year struggle, the women of Utah won back the right to vote.

Catt in Colorado

In 1893, after suffragists were successfully able to pressure the Colorado state legislature to put the issue of women's suffrage on the ballot, they had only five months to mount a campaign. Susan B. Anthony sent Carrie Chapman Catt, a dynamic speaker and the most effective organizer in the national movement.

Catt arrived in Colorado to head the campaign six weeks before the election. Aware of the high unemployment rate in Colorado, she decided to give out free soup.

With each bowl, she handed out literature on women's suffrage.

Packing as much work as she could into the short time before the election, Catt scheduled the speeches so tightly that just getting to the next one on time was sometimes a problem. Catt was a tireless campaigner, whose efforts proved effective.

WCTU Joins the Colorado Campaign

Women's clubs had aroused public awareness about the suffrage issue in Colorado even before Catt's arrival. The Women's Christian Temperance Union (WCTU) also joined the Colorado suffrage movement.

Temperance supporters thought the prohibition of liquor was as necessary as ending child labor and excessive working hours. Appalled by the harm that drunken men had done to women and children, the WCTU saw prohibition of alcohol as the solution to problems of abuse. Many women jumped on the suffrage bandwagon because they wanted to vote for prohibition.

Some suffragists welcomed the WCTU to the fight. Others worried that the "wets"—those who opposed prohibition—would not support women's suffrage if they thought it would mean they could not have a glass of wine or beer with their dinner.

The temperance women were often better organized than the suffragists and better able to spread information. The suffragists were reluctant to give the WCTU workers too much credit, however, because they did not want to alienate the wets.

The Denver liquor dealers, however, had but one cause—to keep alcohol legal—and they mounted their own anti-suffrage campaign. They warned saloon keepers and as many of their patrons as possible that if women got the vote, alcohol would be outlawed. They offered free drinks to unemployed miners and printed circulars that attacked equal suffrage and the women who advocated it.

However, their spirited opposition was no match for the energy of the campaign led by Catt. Voters passed the women's suffrage referendum in 1893. Colorado became the first state to pass women's voting rights by a popular vote.

Why the West?

The reasons women in the West were the first to vote are complex, but some conditions unique to the western states contributed to the advancement of women's rights in the region:

- Women's suffrage was seen as a means for attracting investors or settlers, especially women, to the Wild West.
- Because these areas were in the process of forming governments, which the eastern states had done decades earlier, the question of who would have the vote had to be answered in their new laws. They were forced to think about the issue of women's suffrage.
- The transcontinental railroad, completed in 1869, made the movement of both people and ideas faster, and eastern suffragists, who were well organized, kept the issue alive in the West.[2]

- Finally, because of the physical challenges of being in the unsettled western frontier, women were often more readily accepted when filling traditional male roles. Women commonly helped care for family farms and businesses, and were respected for their work both inside and outside the home.

All of these factors helped women in the American West gain the right to vote much more quickly than women in the more old fashioned East. As the frontier expanded, to an extent so, too, did the rights granted to women pioneers.

Chapter 5

SOME RIGHTS EXTENDED

*D*isfranchisement is largely responsible for [women's] industrial inequality and therefore for the degradation of many women, and we advocate . . . "Equal Pay for Equal Work."[1]

—Fourth Resolution, 1894 convention of the National American Woman Suffrage Association

Widening Horizons

During the last quarter of the nineteenth century, women's lives began to change. The boundaries of the traditional woman's sphere, which had been clearly defined as being the home, were expanding. Some of the rights that Susan B. Anthony had talked about fifty years before were extended to women in a few states. In some northeastern states, women could hold property in their own names and had rights to their own earnings. Female enrollment in high schools was increasing, and the doors to private and public colleges and universities were opening wider.

Demand for women in the workforce offered new choices and opportunities.

The changes began during the Civil War. The military was taking able-bodied men away from the workforce at a time when more goods and services were required to fuel the war effort. It became essential for women to work where they had not been accepted before. They worked in railroads and factories; they collected streetcar fares and ran elevators; they did office jobs previously done only by men.

After the war, factories and businesses that had supplied the military sought new outlets for their goods and services. The resulting increase in mass production and marketing of household goods made women's domestic chores easier.

The birthrate began to decline, which increased women's leisure time. They spent a smaller portion of their lives bearing and rearing children. Though many factors contributed to the decline in births, changing attitudes and expectations of women were among the most important. There were no safe or effective methods of birth control, so many women controlled the size of their families by abortion as well as by other methods. Self-induced abortion had been a common practice for centuries. Interviews at the turn of the twentieth century suggest that abortion and other birth control techniques were common among women of all classes.[2]

Rearing children also took less time because of the new availability of day nurseries, playgrounds, kindergartens, and recreational facilities for children. Women with more leisure time could learn and think about the ideas and issues that the early feminists had talked about. They became increasingly aware that they had the right to make decisions about their own lives. They also sought to broaden their range of interests. One way they did this was to organize clubs, revolving around every interest from hobbies to the controversial social issues of the day.

The Anti-suffragists

Some club activities centered on urban problems. As the idea of women's voting became more acceptable, some club members believed problems could be resolved only by acquiring suffrage and participation in the political process.

However, not all women's clubs supported the suffrage movement. At its 1888 meeting, the International Council of Women did not include suffrage in its statement of goals; nor did the National Council of Women. The General Federation of Women's Clubs did not officially support suffrage until 1914.

Many women saw the campaign for the vote as an attack on what middle-class Americans held dear. The anti-suffragists, called antis, mounted a defense based on a sentimental vision of mother, home, God, and the Constitution. They said that women's place in the home was determined by sex, not individual abilities or wishes. According to the antis, women were destined from birth to be full-time mothers and wives.

Antis argued that voting was much more complicated than just putting a ballot in a box once in a while. It required becoming politically informed. If this happened, they warned, it would lead to the inevitable: Discussions between spouses on the issues could lead to disagreements, and that could end in divorce.

In addition to increasing the divorce rate, antis also warned that juvenile delinquency would increase because politically active mothers would neglect their children. Women would eventually be drawn to political organization, and then into public office. Antis argued that sex should not be injected into politics—which meant politics should remain male only.

Some antis favored women's involvement if it included only nonpartisan political activity (not on the side of one party against the other). But they opposed suffrage because they believed it "would dispel women's energies and dilute their influence."[3] They did not argue that women did not have a right to involvement outside the home; they just narrowly defined that involvement.

Suffragists argued that antis put women in the same category as idiots, aliens, and criminals—other groups of people who could not vote. Antis countered by saying that it was incorrect to say women did not have the right to vote, like those groups. Rather, women had the right *not* to vote. Women were not "deprived" of the privilege to vote, but were instead "exempt" from the burden of it.[4] In other words, the antis argued that women were lucky not to be involved in the tiresome business of politics and government.

Suffrage Groups Unite

In addition to the rise of women's clubs and the anti-suffrage movement, the latter part of the nineteenth century saw unification of the two main suffrage groups. Alice Stone Blackwell, the only daughter of Lucy Stone and Henry Blackwell, helped bring about the reunion of the National Woman Suffrage Association (NWSA) and the American Woman Suffrage Association (AWSA).

Alice Stone Blackwell, sometimes called the foremost suffrage propagandist, was the editor of *Woman's Journal*, a weekly newspaper her parents had founded and managed with the financial and political backing of New England reformers. It was the main publication of the AWSA and became the official paper of the combined groups after the merger. Its masthead declared, "Devoted to the Interests of Woman, to her Education, Industrial, Legal and Political Equality and especially her right to Suffrage."[5]

When Alice Stone Blackwell was corresponding secretary of the AWSA, she proposed a meeting of the two organizations to consider a merger. At its fall 1887 convention, the AWSA resolved that Lucy Stone would confer with Susan B. Anthony of the NWSA to consider a possible reunion.

On December 21, 1887, Susan B. Anthony, Lucy Stone, Alice Stone Blackwell, and Rachel Foster, a young apprentice to Anthony, met in Boston to discuss unification.

The two wings negotiated for two years before the merger became final. The two groups met publicly for the first time on February 18, 1890, and elected Elizabeth Cady Stanton president and Anthony vice president at large. They declared themselves the National American Woman Suffrage Association (NAWSA). The movement seemed to be united at last.

AFRICAN-AMERICAN SUFFRAGISTS

There is a great stir about colored men getting their rights, but not a word about the colored women; and if colored men get their rights, and not colored women theirs, you see the colored men will be masters over the women, and it will be just as bad as it was before. . . . Now if you want me to get out of the world, you had better get the women votin' soon.[1]

—Sojourner Truth

Black Women Discarded

Before the Civil War, black and white women had worked together to abolish slavery. After the war, they worked side by side for universal suffrage in the American Equal Rights Association.

They were divided bitterly, however, in 1869, when women were excluded from the Fourteenth and Fifteenth amendments and the two major women's suffrage organizations went their separate ways. The American Woman Suffrage Association remained sympathetic to African-

American women, and many were counted among its membership. The National Woman Suffrage Association, instead, attempted to focus on suffrage only and moved away from the needs of African-American women.

Once the two factions reunited to form the National American Woman Suffrage Association (NAWSA), the leaders focused on winning the vote and avoided all causes they thought radical. They put more distance between women's rights and the rights of African Americans.

There were several reasons behind this turnabout. Many white suffragists were angry because black men had been allowed to vote before they were. Some were also disturbed by the fact that male immigrants—many in the country for only a short time—could vote while white American-born women could not. Also, NAWSA's newest members were more conservative, and the organization catered to them in order to keep them in its ranks.

NAWSA's new strategy also included gaining support in the South. The suffragists' previous connection with abolition proved to be a problem now that white conservatives again controlled the region.

To gain acceptance, a Southern strategy was formulated. NAWSA leaders argued that women's suffrage would not endanger white supremacy in the South, but would restore it. They suggested attaching property or educational qualifications to women's suffrage, which would disqualify most black women from voting. The South could then maintain white supremacy in politics.[2]

During the late nineteenth and early twentieth centuries, white suffragists mainly ignored African-American women. Despite the huge obstacles they faced, though, African-American suffragists played an active role in the fight for suffrage. If the vote was necessary to protect white women's rights, then black women, who faced racism as well as sexism, needed it even more.[3]

After their freedom had been won, African Americans in the United States lived in terrible poverty; worked long hours at hard, menial jobs; and faced discrimination, physical threats, and violence. Survival—for themselves and their families—was a daily battle. Even so, more and more African-American women found the time and energy to demand the right to vote.

Sojourner Truth

During the mid-nineteenth century, African-American suffragists' speeches were rarely written down, so there is little evidence of their views today. One exception was Sojourner Truth, whose words of wisdom were so colorful that they caught the ear of white suffrage leaders and were frequently recorded. Unlike the majority of other African-American suffrage leaders, Truth was an illiterate, freed slave who did menial labor to support herself. Most other African-American women leaders were literate, privileged, and had been born free.

A series of women's conventions across the country followed the 1848 convention in Seneca Falls. At a convention in 1851, Truth delivered an eloquent speech that still echoes in the hearts of women of all colors. Tall and thin, wearing a white turban and a gray dress, Truth stood before the mostly white group and said:

That man over there says that women need to be helped into carriages and lifted over ditches. . . . Nobody ever helps me into carriages, or over mud-puddles or gives me any best place. And a'n't I a woman?

Look at me! Look at my arm. I have plowed, and planted, and gathered into barns, and no man could head me! And a'n't I a woman?[4]

In the antislavery movement, black women faced discrimination on three levels: being abolitionists in a slave society; being black among white reformers; and being women in a movement dominated by men.[5]

Parallel Paths

Like their white counterparts, black suffragists split on ideology after the ratification of the Fourteenth and Fifteenth Amendments. The disagreements were similar. Some thought the word *male* should not have been included in the Fourteenth Amendment; others thought it was right to first enfranchise African-American men and then fight for women's right to vote.

As in the white suffrage movement, some African-American leaders argued that the Fifteenth Amendment should apply to women because it did not exclude them by definition of citizenship. Frances Harper, along with other black suffragists, led debates and discussions on this idea.

Harper, a poet, was freeborn. She had supported herself from the age of thirteen by working as a nurse-maid, by lecturing on abolition, and by doing public readings of her poetry. In the 1890s, she wrote the first novel ever published in the United States by an African-American woman, *Iola Leroy, or Shadows Uplifted.*

In the 1890s, a growing number of African-American women organized, in part, because more of the children—the first generation born out of slavery—were educated. In 1896, the National Association of Colored Women (NACW) was formed by Frances Harper and Mary Church Terrell. The NACW connected African-American women across the nation. By the 1920s, it had as many as two hundred thousand members in forty-one states.[6]

Mary Church Terrell

A college graduate and an educator, Terrell was elected the first president of the NACW. She, along with other black female leaders, included suffrage in her campaign to lead black women to self-help. The problems of black women differed from those of white women. Native-born white women did not have their dignity routinely trampled as black women did. Whites were not accused of being wanton, immoral, and socially inferior because of their skin color. They did not face racial discrimination in employment and education.

Although black women were excluded from most white women's organizations in 1898, they were not formally excluded from NAWSA. So, Terrell submitted a resolution to the organization that stated a variety of injustices to which black people were routinely subjected. The resolution was adopted by the national organization, but groups remained opposed to addressing racial issues on the local level.

Susan B. Anthony spoke of racial equality, but she continued to support separation of race and suffrage as the political strategy for NAWSA's platform. This left potential for bigotry in the organization and kept African-American feminists on the outskirts of the movement.

Ida B. Wells-Barnett

In 1913, journalist Ida B. Wells-Barnett, a prominent black suffragist, organized the Alpha Suffrage Club, the first women's club for African Americans in Chicago. Its purpose was to act as a liaison with other state and national organizations to show women how getting the right to vote would help them.

That same year, when she tried to take her place as representative of her club in a women's suffrage parade, she was told she would have to go to the back of the parade with the rest of the African-American women. She refused and disappeared into the crowd. As the parade began, she slipped out of the crowd and walked between two white Illinois delegates who were sympathetic to her.

A photograph of Wells-Barnett between the two women appeared in *The Chicago Daily Tribune* and served as a reminder that even though NAWSA tried to separate the issues, the "negro question" and women's suffrage were inseparable.

Racism Within

When Fannie Barrier Williams, an African-American club member in Chicago, attempted to join the Chicago Woman's Club in 1894, the all-white group was divided on admitting her. After fourteen months of debate, she was finally allowed to join.

Josephine St. Pierre Ruffin, a black woman who was once described as playing a leading role in every movement to emancipate black women, started her suffrage activities in 1875. Throughout the 1890s, she urged white and black women to unite. But at the General Federation of Women's Clubs in Wisconsin in 1900, the club she officially represented stated "that colored women should confine themselves to their clubs and the large field of work open to them there."[7]

Susan B. Anthony's abolitionist background and personal friendships with African-American activists took a backseat to the priority of women's suffrage. She asked Frederick Douglass, a former slave and exceptional speaker and writer, not to attend the 1895 NAWSA convention. She feared his presence would offend the Southern hosts.[8]

At the 1903 NAWSA convention in New Orleans, Louisiana, the national organization's stand was to give states the right to develop their own positions. Despite the devoted efforts of African-American women, the position taken by many white suffrage leaders was basically an endorsement of white supremacy, especially in the South. For African-American suffragists, the struggle to be seen as equals would continue.

FRACTURED

Our religion, laws, customs are all founded on the belief that woman was made for man. . . . How this marriage question grows on me. It lies at the very foundation of all progress. . . . My own life . . . brought me to the conclusion. So fear not that I shall falter. I shall not grow conservative with age.[1]

—Elizabeth Cady Stanton

Anthony and Stanton Disagree

Combining the two suffrage organizations into NAWSA signified unity in the battle. But with unity came conservatism and an objection to dissent. This created an atmosphere unwelcome to Elizabeth Cady Stanton, the movement's philosopher.

Though their love and friendship never changed, Stanton and Susan B. Anthony began to grow apart in their political ideas. Stanton did not agree with Anthony's nonpartisan strategy for winning outside support, and she wanted more discussion within the organization.

She saw that suffragists disagreed on how to use the vote to gain political, religious, social, educational, and industrial rights. Rather than attempt to present a united front on these issues, Stanton wanted an open debate.

But it was Stanton's critique of Christianity that caused the greatest problem within NAWSA. Though Stanton had always been critical of the Christian religion, the issue became more important to her in her later years.

Among other issues, Stanton argued that Christianity taught hostility toward women by defining men as heads of families. She charged that the spread of Christianity had lowered women's position in society.[2]

Because of Stanton's radical ideas and anti-Christian opinions, she became unpopular among many feminists. In 1892, after serving only two years, she resigned from her position as NAWSA president. "It is not good for all our thoughts or interests to run in one groove. For this reason I resigned the office I held," she said in a letter to a friend.[3] Anthony took up the reins.

Although it was difficult for Anthony to admit it, her viewpoint was becoming quite different from that of her dear friend. She once portrayed herself as being dependent upon Stanton's intellect.[4] But Anthony had since discovered her own political path, and, to her dismay, it diverged from Stanton's.

Through it all, however, their friendship did not waver. Anthony once said:

> I never expect to know any joy in this world equal to that of going up and down the land, getting good editorials written, engaging halls and circulating Mrs. Stanton's speeches. If I ever have had any inspiration she has given it to me, for I never could have done my work if I had not had this woman at my right hand.[5]

When Stanton died in 1902, Anthony was stunned. When pressed by reporters for a comment, she could only say: "I cannot express myself at all as I feel, I am too crushed to speak. If I had died first she would have found beautiful phrases to describe our friendship, but I cannot put it into words."[6]

Harriot Stanton Blatch

Stanton's daughter, Harriot Stanton Blatch, was born in 1856 in Seneca Falls, New York, the birthplace of the suffrage movement. She had educational opportunities of which her mother had only dreamed: She graduated from Vassar College with honors in mathematics; she studied in Paris and in Berlin; and she earned a master of arts degree.

Harriot married an Englishman in 1882 and lived in England for twenty years. During that time, British women were battling for the right to vote. Harriot Blatch's association with Emmeline Pankhurst, a militant British suffragist, and the British suffrage movement would have a significant effect on the direction in which she and other young women took the United States suffrage movement.

When Blatch returned to live in the United States, she organized street meetings and parades in New York City.

She agreed with the philosophy of a group she had joined while in England, that the lower classes could be led forward by reformers.

In 1907, Blatch organized the Equality League of Self-Supporting Women in New York, part of a large network of NAWSA organizations. The league, later called the Women's Political Union (WPU), was patterned after the Women's Social and Political Union of England led by Pankhurst. It was one of many new clubs organized along political lines to more effectively influence legislators and party organizations on the local level.

In 1910, the WPU organized a series of parades in New York City. Conservative suffrage leaders objected, fearing that radical demonstrations would set the movement back.[7] But hundreds of women marched down the streets of New York City, booed by some and cheered by others. These marches produced one of the most lingering images of the movement.

Five More States

The combining of the two suffrage organizations into NAWSA resulted in a consensus among leaders of the suffrage movement that the only way to get an amendment to the United States Constitution was to win the vote in a significant number of states first. They reasoned that once a majority of states had approved state amendments, passage of a federal amendment would not be difficult.

Suffragists had been mired in a fourteen-year drought between 1896, when Utah and Idaho women won suffrage, and 1910, when the right to vote was achieved by

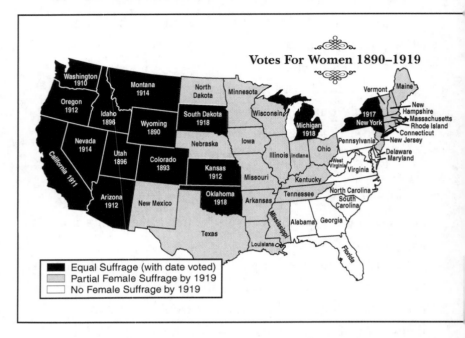

The struggle for women's right to vote took many years, with states gradually giving women suffrage at different times.

women in Washington State. They referred to this period as the doldrums.

Their success in the State of Washington was attributable to the support of labor unions and progressives and the absence of an organized opposition. Before the territory became a state, women had twice won the vote, then twice lost it in the territory's supreme court.

Emma Smith DeVoe, who led the Washington campaign, woke Carrie Chapman Catt, chair of NAWSA's organizing committee, in 1910 with a telephone call to give her the good news: "The State of Washington has voted woman suffrage, two to one!" There was silence. Catt hesitated, then replied, "I can stand defeat, but victory is almost too much for me!"[8]

The Washington victory and new strategies in the East, which suffragists borrowed from their more militant British sisters, created a resurgence of energy and enthusiasm. Another element made its way across the ocean—the term *suffragette*. It was a term used in England for women activists because of their youth—many were university students. The older American women were insulted when the press used the term in reference to them. They considered it patronizing and preferred to be called suffragists.[9]

The militant-aggressive tone set by the WPU in New York was duplicated, helping to win suffrage in California in 1911.[10]

Women in Arizona, Oregon, and Kansas also won the right to vote when those states passed state constitutional amendments in 1912. The state-by-state campaign was moving full speed ahead.

NEW CENTURY, OLD BATTLE

*N*o *matter what is done or is not done, how you are criticized or misunderstood, or what efforts are made to block your path, remember that the only fear you need have is the fear of not standing by the thing you believe to be right. Take your stand and hold it: then let come what will, and receive the blows like a good soldier.*[1]

—Susan B. Anthony

New Leadership

Around 1900, both Susan B. Anthony and Elizabeth Cady Stanton were in their eighties. A new generation of women, led by Harriot Stanton Blatch, Carrie Chapman Catt, and Anna Howard Shaw, took the reins to lead the women's movement into the new century.

Before Anthony chose the woman she would endorse to succeed her as president of NAWSA, she had narrowed the decision to Catt and Shaw. Shaw wanted the job. She said her "highest ambition had been to succeed Miss

Anthony, for no one who knew her as I did could underestimate the honor of being chosen by her to carry on her work."[2]

Short and stocky with dark eyes and an expressive face, Anna Howard Shaw was an ordained minister and a doctor, both rare accomplishments for women at the turn of the twentieth century. She was recognized as a great orator with the ability to move audiences.

Born in England, Shaw had come to the United States as a child and grew up in the backwoods of Michigan. As a youth, she decided she wanted to become a minister. Over the objections of her family, she worked her way through college and then attended Boston University's theological school, where she was the only woman in her class.

She graduated in 1880 and was ordained by the Methodist Protestant Church. She served as pastor of two Massachusetts churches. Horrified by the number of sick people she saw in the slums of Boston, she went back to school to study medicine and earned a degree in 1885.

She became involved with the suffrage movement through her work as a lecturer for the Women's Christian Temperance Union. She would later become a devoted friend of Susan B. Anthony.

During the International Council of Women in 1888, Shaw preached the Sunday sermon. Anthony, on her way back to her room after one of the evening meetings, was thinking about Shaw's dedication to women and her powerful preaching. Nearing her seventies, Anthony was searching for someone who could follow in her footsteps.

On the spur of the moment, she decided to pay a visit to Shaw before retiring for the night.

"I had gone to bed—indeed, I was almost asleep when she came, for the day had been as exhausting as it was interesting," Shaw said. Anthony informed Shaw that she had a lot to say. She sat in an easy chair, put a blanket around her knees, and began talking. She "talked of the Cause—always the Cause—and what we must do for it," Shaw said. When the light of morning came through the windows, Anthony was surprised. "My we seemed to have talked all night," she said. She stood up, told Shaw that she must go dress for a morning meeting, and suggested that Shaw get herself a cup of coffee.[3]

In the end, Anthony did not choose Shaw to be her successor. She decided on Carrie Chapman Catt, the most effective organizer in the movement. Catt served for four years, from 1900 to 1904. When she resigned—due to her husband's ill health—Shaw took her place and served as president of NAWSA until 1915.

During her presidency, Shaw became Anthony's closest friend and was with Anthony when she died. On her deathbed, Anthony made Shaw promise that she would keep the presidency as long as she was well enough to work. Shaw asked how she could keep that promise, considering she served by the election of those around her. "Promise to make them wish you to keep it . . . remain until the friends you most trust tell you it is time to withdraw. . . . Promise me that."[4]

Shaw's promise was the last thing Anthony heard before she passed into unconsciousness. She died on

March 13, 1906. Ten thousand mourners passed by the simple Quaker casket as twelve women dressed in white stood guard around it. Women students attending the University of Rochester in New York served as honor bearers. They wore the full commencement dress, including black academic gowns and mortarboards. They carried the flowers that had been sent to Anthony's home and escorted family and friends behind the casket during the funeral procession.

Shaw offered the final remarks: "There is no death for such as she. There are no last words of love. The ages to come will revere her name. Unnumbered generations of the children of men shall rise up to call her blessed . . . for never did a more victorious hero enter into rest."[5]

At Anthony's death, women in only four states— Wyoming, Utah, Idaho, and Colorado—had won the right to vote.

Liquor Forces

The liquor industry was a formidable foe of the suffrage movement. Catt called it the Invisible Enemy.[6] Even though alcoholic beverages were legal—the Eighteenth Amendment prohibiting the sale and distribution of alcoholic beverages did not take effect until 1920—the liquor industry tied together women's voting rights and prohibition. Men were warned that if women were allowed to vote, all their liquor would be taken away. And because leaders in the suffrage movement—Anthony, Stanton, Catt, and Shaw—all came to the suffrage battle via the temperance movement, it was an easy, though inaccurate, assumption to make.

In 1917 in Ohio, liquor interests teamed with antis— opponents of women's suffrage—after a bill was passed that granted women the right to vote in presidential elections. They circulated petitions to have the issue referred to voters for repeal.

Saloons gathered most of the signatures by keeping the petitions on the bars. Men certified names by declaring they had witnessed the signatures, which would have been impossible unless they had been in the bar eighteen hours a day for several weeks. According to the dates on some petitions, they were circulated by the same men on the same day in different counties. Some petitions had names only, no addresses; and some had whole pages of signatures in the same handwriting.

The Ohio suffragists challenged the petitions as fraudulent but were able to secure hearings in only four counties. In those four, 8,661 of the 9,964 signatures were declared fraudulent and thrown out. But it was not enough to block the referendum. The wets won. The action of the legislature to grant women the vote was reversed.[7]

Complaints of fraud in referendums in Michigan, Nebraska, and Iowa were proven, but recounts were denied.

Another tactic of liquor interests was to challenge laws in the courts that granted women the right to vote. When

South Dakota became a state in 1889, prohibition was adopted there, and liquor forces were anxious to repeal it. They viewed the proposed state suffrage amendment of 1890 as protection of prohibition and fought to defeat it also. The amendment was defeated, as it would be five more times. The campaign for women's suffrage was not successful in South Dakota until 1918.

For good or for bad, the women's suffrage movement would remain closely tied to the temperance movement in the eyes of the public for many years.

NEW TACTICS

I always have been a suffragist, but I never got the spirit of this thing till I saw that parade, yesterday. This is not a movement; it is not a campaign; this is a crusade![1]

—Henry Allen, governor of Kansas, 1919–1923

Militancy

Alice Paul, who was an instrumental force in the battle for suffrage, was a Quaker like Susan B. Anthony. When Paul was asked what had converted her to the suffrage cause, she said that she could not remember a time when she did not believe in it. "You know the Quakers have always believed in Woman Suffrage," she said.[2]

Paul, born in 1885 in New Jersey, earned a bachelor's degree, a master's degree, and a doctorate in sociology. She then went to study in England, where she met Lucy Burns. A Brooklyn native who had graduated from Vassar College, Burns was a student at the University of Bonn, Germany, when they met. Burns visited England on vacation and joined the suffrage movement within a few weeks. In the years to come, the two friends would share many experiences, including arrests, imprisonment, and hunger strikes.

When Burns returned to the United States in the summer of 1912, Alice Paul, who had left England in 1910, approached her with the idea of moving to Washington, D.C., to work for passage of a federal constitutional amendment. Paul believed continued work on state-by-state campaigns was a waste of time.[3]

On January 2, 1913, Paul and Lucy Burns established the Washington, D.C., headquarters of the NAWSA Congressional Committee.

Parades to Persuade

Paul was adept at keeping the issue of suffrage in the news. As chair of the Congressional Committee, she raised the money needed to open the office and finance a parade to coincide with the presidential inauguration of Woodrow Wilson.

On March 3, 1913, one day before Wilson's inauguration, eight thousand to ten thousand women and men marched down Pennsylvania Avenue. *The New York Times* said, "The capital saw the greatest parade of women in its history."[4]

Prominent suffragist Inez Milholland led the parade, wearing flowing white robes and riding a white horse. She was followed by thousands of suffragists, some in costumes and many with banners. Floats illustrated the history of the movement. Nearly every state in the Union was represented by marchers, banners, and signs.

An estimated five hundred thousand people watched. The unfriendly crowd surged forward constantly and in many places broke the ropes that had been stretched to keep it back. At times the marchers had to walk in a narrow line, and several times they were stopped while policemen and a mounted escort pushed back the shouting spectators.

The marchers walked calmly and kept a military formation whenever they could. Some in the crowd attacked the marchers, spat on them, and threw lit cigars at them. Hundreds of marchers were injured. Finally, the United States Cavalry was called in to restore order. Harriot Stanton Blatch accused the government of leaving the women at the mercy of a howling mob.

Since some congressmen and their wives were among the marchers, the outrageous attacks by the mob led to a congressional investigation. This resulted in the removal of the capital's chief of police. The affair received massive press coverage.

Though this was one of the most dramatic and grandest parades for suffrage, it was not the first, and it would not be the last. Hundreds of parades across the nation kept the issue in the public eye.

Paul and Shaw Split

Under Alice Paul's leadership, NAWSA's Congressional Committee changed from an ineffective one—as it had been under Anna Howard Shaw's presidency—to a successful lobbying center. Still, Paul became impatient because the committee had to answer to NAWSA, which she considered too conservative. She did not agree with NAWSA's variety of approaches, including state-by-state campaigns. She was convinced that the road to victory would be a single-minded campaign to secure passage of an amendment to the United States Constitution.

Alice Paul, with Lucy Burns's help, organized the Congressional Union (CU) in April 1913. The CU was still affiliated with NAWSA, but unlike the Congressional Committee, its sole purpose was to lobby for a national suffrage amendment. Paul served as president of the CU while still chair of NAWSA's Congressional Committee.

In the beginning, the CU operated with the approval of Anna Shaw and NAWSA. But it quickly assumed a different identity—based on Paul's philosophy—and pursued policies that were not approved by NAWSA. In the summer of 1914, Paul urged that direct pressure be applied to the Democratic Party, then in power. She orchestrated campaigns to vote Democrats out of office. Shaw, on the other hand, wanted to cultivate relationships with the Democrats, not vote them out.

The CU did its own fundraising and spent its own funds, which were not funneled through the national organization's treasury. However, since the CU used NAWSA stationery to raise money and recruit members, the NAWSA board wanted the CU to follow its agenda. The CU would not. In 1914, Paul, considered by some a dangerous radical, was asked to resign as chair of the Congressional Committee. She complied, but she took the CU with her.

By this time, Paul and Burns had gathered support, mainly from suffragists who were impatient with the slow progress of the national association. Shaw disliked Paul and blamed herself for not reining her in earlier, before Paul had won supporters. But Shaw was especially disappointed with Paul's followers, whom she called "blank fools" for being influenced to follow the more radical arm of the movement.[5]

In March 1917, the CU was renamed the National Woman's Party (NWP), as it struck out independently under the leadership of Alice Paul.

Chapter 10

ANOTHER WAR

Success will depend less on the money we are able to command, than upon our combined ability to lift the campaign above this sordidness of mind, and to elevate it to the position of a crusade for human freedom.[1]

—Carrie Chapman Catt

The Plan

Carrie Chapman Catt, long recognized as NAWSA's best organizer, took back the title of president after Anna Howard Shaw resigned in 1915. Catt's organizational skills brought new energy to the stalled movement.

Catt unveiled what she called The Plan, also known as The Winning Plan, at an emergency NAWSA convention in 1916. Pressured by Alice Paul and by impatience within NAWSA itself, Catt planned to drop the state-by-state emphasis and push for a national constitutional amendment.

Catt's plan came at a price. Catt had to build support for the shift in strategy. Opposition from the Southern representatives was significant. The South strongly supported states' rights and fought hard against anything it perceived as attempted control by the federal government.

The Rift Grows

Paul and the National Woman's Party (NWP) blamed the party in power for the fact that women did not have the right to vote. Following the United States' entry into World War I in April 1917, the NWP argued that before the nation fought for freedom on foreign soil, freedom at home should be addressed.

The NWP used acts of civil disobedience (nonviolent opposition to a law by refusing to comply with it) to focus attention on the issue. Paul and her followers began picketing the White House and getting arrested. It was the first time suffragists had taken their public demonstrations to the president's front gate.

Catt thought picketing brought more problems than solutions. Many viewed the pickets as militant and criticized their behavior. NAWSA, under Catt's leadership, published objections to the picketing tactic in 350 newspapers across the country, referring to the pickets as a tiny minority.[2]

Catt urged Paul to withdraw the pickets and expressed her belief that picketing was hurting the movement. But Paul held fast. She believed their efforts were revitalizing and publicizing the push for an amendment.

The rift between the two women continued to grow.

Iron-Jawed Angels

The Congressional Union (CU), under Alice Paul's leadership, carried on a variety of activities to keep the issue of women's voting rights in the public eye. From 1913 to 1917, CU members circulated petitions, organized an automobile procession across the country, and sent delegates to influence statesmen. They organized parades and pageants, kept hectic speaking schedules, and heckled President Wilson's speeches whenever possible. They lobbied Congress and attended committee hearings and political conventions. They interviewed candidates and campaigned against the Democrats.

The "silent sentinels," as the pickets were called because they rarely spoke, changed hourly, the new team marching out of NWP headquarters, through Lafayette Square, and to the gates of the White House.[3] During World War I, the pickets' banners became even more critical of Wilson's administration. The banners claimed that the United States, fighting a war for freedom in Europe, was not democratic. The pickets were becoming an even greater embarrassment to the administration.

In June 1917, the pickets faced mob attacks and charges. Picketers were arrested for obstructing traffic. Refusing to pay fines, they were jailed.

The pickets walked back and forth in front of the White House gates in groups of four. As quickly as one group of four was arrested, another group was sent out. It was a continuous picket line.

Lucy Burns and newspaper writer Peggy Baird Johns served sixty-day sentences at a workhouse. In September, they drafted a letter to the district commissioners in Washington, demanding to be considered political prisoners. They said they were political offenders, not traffic obstructors, as charged. That status would not have changed their situation, but it would have made a statement. The embarrassment to the government would have been enormous if they had been declared political prisoners. Their letter was never answered.

In addition to arrests, President Wilson's advisor Joseph Tumulty suggested a press blackout of stories about the NWP. Publicity was essential to the NWP militancy plan. It was media coverage that had sparked public sympathy, support, and even outrage. The Washington newspapers agreed, and by mid-1917 they rarely covered NWP activities. When they did report on the demonstrations, it was not in a favorable manner.[4]

Night of Terror

On November 14, 1917, thirty-three NWP members were arrested for picketing the White House. They became victims of what has become known as the night of terror.[5] The violence began when two soldiers jabbed a picket between the eyes with her broken, splintered banner. Another picket was knocked around by three youths.

After the women were arrested, they were taken to the workhouse. One suffragist was clubbed in her cell. When the other women feared that she had suffered a heart attack, their pleas to the guards were ignored. She lived, as did the climate of fear.

Burns, a vocal leader, was treated especially harshly. She was beaten and her wrists were handcuffed high on her cell door.

Guards roughed up a woman who was trying to pull away from them. They pinched her arms and twisted her wrists as they wrestled her down over an iron bench. One guard grabbed her by the throat.

No one received treatment for injuries. The women were not even allowed to use the toilet throughout the night.

As the news of their treatment filtered out, the public became enraged. Nine days after the picketers were arrested, Judge Edmund Waddill decided the women had been committed to the workhouse illegally and instead they should be taken to the district jail. On November 27 and 28, all the women arrested on the night of terror were pardoned by President Wilson and released.

The night of terror did not stop the women from picketing. Unjust imprisonment had left its mark, making the women more radical. They had believed in the promise of democracy. After being jailed for what they saw as an exercise of freedom of speech, they viewed their society differently. Rather than draw back from militancy, they approached it with renewed energy.[6]

Silent Sentinels

The picketing continued. The silent sentinels—a quiet but visual reminder—made it impossible for Wilson to leave or enter the White House without seeing them and their banners.

President Wilson finally endorsed the Nineteenth Amendment, which granted women's suffrage, and the House passed it in 1918. But in early 1919, with the Senate still one vote away, the suffragists put even more pressure on Wilson to use his influence to get it passed. His endorsement of the amendment made no difference constitutionally and was seen by some as an improper action for a president to take. Still, suffragists reasoned that his endorsement could influence the vote of some senators.

In January 1919, the NWP lighted a "perpetual fire of freedom" in front of the White House.[7] The suffragists stood guard over the fire throughout the night. When hostile observers broke the flaming urn, the women replaced it and rebuilt the fire. They were arrested, charged with violating a law that prohibited outdoor fires between sunset and sunrise.

Other demonstrations continued. A group of suffragists burned parts of Wilson's speeches that dealt with either democracy or liberty. Women who had been in prison, "jailed for freedom," as they called it, wore replicas of their prison uniforms and toured the country on a train dubbed the Prison Special.[8]

Then, in March 1919, at what would be the NWP's last militant protest before passage of the national amendment, violence broke out. Wilson was scheduled to speak at the New York Metropolitan Opera House shortly after Congress had adjourned without a Senate vote on the amendment. Twenty-five women marched toward the opera house with banners protesting Wilson's "autocracy" (dictatorship).[9]

They were met by two hundred policemen. A crowd of mostly sailors and soldiers joined the police, rushed the women, and beat them back. The clash lasted for hours. Women were clubbed, knocked down, and trampled. Many were bleeding from their faces and hands; their arms were bruised and twisted. Some of the women were near unconsciousness. Purses and wristwatches were stolen.

The suffragists were arrested and charged with disorderly conduct and assaulting the police. Then they were released. The new militant strategy had again ended in violence.

FINAL BATTLE

*F*ailure is impossible![1]

—Susan B. Anthony's last public words.

Congressional Journey

The first joint resolution of the women's suffrage amendment was proposed in Congress in 1878. It read: "The right of citizens of the United States to vote shall not be denied or abridged by the United States or by any State on account of sex."[2] If it had been passed, it would have become the Sixteenth Amendment to the Constitution of the United States.

Instead, the Sixteenth Amendment, passed in 1913, granted Congress the power to tax personal income. The Seventeenth Amendment, also passed in 1913, gave citizens the power to elect their United States senators directly. Prior to passage of this amendment, state legislatures chose members of the United States Senate.

Alcoholic drinks were banned by passage of the Eighteenth Amendment. Ratified in 1919, it became law in 1920 and made it illegal to make or sell alcoholic beverages in the United States. Prohibition, as this law was called, ended fourteen years later when the Twenty-first Amendment was passed.

On January 10, 1918, a vote on the Susan B. Anthony amendment for women's suffrage was scheduled in the House of Representatives. The galleries were packed when the House convened at noon. Representative Jeannette Rankin of Montana—the first woman ever elected to Congress—opened the debate.

The suffragists needed every favorable vote to make the two-thirds majority required. Three representatives left hospital beds to vote. Another was carried in on a stretcher to cast his vote. A congressmen from the West Coast barely arrived in time to respond to his name during roll call. One left his wife as she lay dying so that he could cast his vote. His wife, a devoted suffragist, died while he was gone.

The women in the gallery checked off each vote on tally sheets. They were aware that if only one vote changed from yea to nay, the amendment would be lost.

The gallery rocked with cheers when the clerk read the result. The amendment had won by one vote. But the rejoicing was short-lived. The suffragists knew they faced an even more difficult battle in the Senate, and to their dismay, the Senate adjourned for the summer without taking action.

When the Senate convened in the fall, President Wilson addressed the senators one day before the scheduled vote and argued for granting women the vote. He urged that the amendment be passed as a war measure as well as for the needs the country would have to address when the war was over.[3]

After he spoke, a senator from Alabama spoke against the amendment. A senator from Missouri continued the opposition by shouting, "A petticoat brigade awaits outside, and Senate leaders like pages trek back and forth for orders!"[4]

The vote fell two short of the required two-thirds majority. Two campaigns were immediately launched: Catt and NAWSA began an attack against the hostile senators; Paul started the watch fires in front of the White House.

The pressure worked. The president personally called senators and urged them to support the amendment. Democratic leaders, embarrassed by the scenes in front of the White House, called a meeting to gain support for the suffrage amendment.

Hoping to stop the demonstrations, the chairman of the Senate Suffrage Committee announced another vote. It was set for February 10, 1919. The amendment was defeated again, this time by one vote.

New Congress

When Congress convened a special session in May 1919, its first order of business was the suffrage amendment. On the third day of the session, the House passed it by a large

majority. Two weeks later, the Senate passed the amendment—on its fifth try since 1887. The women's suffrage
amendment was finally on its way to the states for ratification to become the Nineteenth Amendment.

The suffragists wasted no time celebrating. Less than
an hour after the Senate vote, Carrie Chapman Catt
launched her plan to gain ratification of the Nineteenth
Amendment. Alice Paul had left Washington several days
before the Senate vote to coordinate ratification efforts in
the states whose legislatures were in session.

Road to Ratification

Congress set no time limit on ratification of the amendment, but suffragists were determined to get it done as
quickly as possible. Thirty-six of the forty-eight states
would have to ratify the amendment for it to be added to
the Constitution.

Four states—Illinois, Massachusetts, Pennsylvania,
and Wisconsin—were in regular session. Three states—
Ohio, Michigan, and Texas—were in special session on
other matters. Lobbyists were immediately dispatched to
those states. Campaigners fanned out to the other states to
call for special sessions.

There were two defeats in January 1920—Mississippi
and South Carolina—and two in February—Virginia, for
the second time, and Maryland. Still, the suffragists did
find some success in getting the states to ratify the amendment.

On March 22, 1920, Washington became the last western state and the thirty-fifth state overall to ratify. With

ratification only one state away, the anti-suffragists beefed up their campaign, challenging Ohio's ratification in the courts. The issue went all the way to the United States Supreme Court, which upheld the validity of the Ohio ratification.[5]

Due to a defeat by the Republican-dominated legislature in Delaware, and because Vermont and Connecticut, both Republican-controlled, had not ratified, suffragists staged a demonstration in June 1920 at the Republican National Convention in Chicago. A long line of women, dressed in white and carrying banners with streamers of purple, white, and gold—the crusade's colors—marched from the NWP headquarters to the Coliseum, where the convention was being held. One banner read: WE HAVE HAD ENOUGH RESOLUTIONS. GIVE US THE 36TH STATE. Another said: VOTE AGAINST THE REPUBLICAN PARTY AS LONG AS IT BLOCKS SUFFRAGE. Yet another read: REPUBLICANS WE ARE HERE. WHERE IS THE 36TH STATE?[6] The demonstrators caused Republican leaders to put pressure on the governors of Vermont and Connecticut, but it was to no avail.

After Louisiana and North Carolina also defeated the amendment, suffragists zeroed in on Tennessee.

The Thirty-sixth State

A campaign was launched to press Tennessee Governor A. H. Roberts, a Democrat, to request a special session of the state legislature. The Democratic National Committee passed a resolution asking him to call a special session.

President Wilson sent a telegram urging him to do the same thing.

On the opening day of the Democratic National Convention in San Francisco, Roberts announced that a special session would be held on August 9 in his state. The Tennessee legislature convened, and the state senate ratified the amendment on August 13 by an overwhelming majority, as expected. But passage in the state's house of representatives would be much more difficult.

Many members of the house stayed in Nashville's Hermitage Hotel when the legislature was in session. They were observed frequenting a room on the eighth floor where alcohol was freely served. Catt asked why the prohibition laws were not being enforced. She was told, "In Tennessee whiskey and legislation go hand in hand, especially when controversial questions are urged."[7]

The nine days in Nashville between opening day and ratification in the house were hectic and intense. In addition to suffragists, representing both NAWSA and the NWP, anti-suffrage forces had come to the capital in droves. Suffragists were at the house from morning to night; nothing could be taken for granted from one hour to the next. Just because a house member was for the amendment in the morning did not guarantee he would still be in favor by day's end.

On the morning of the vote, suffragists made sure their legislative friends arrived at the state capitol. As rumors surfaced that some legislators had changed their votes, lobbyists talked to them once again and reminded them that they had made a commitment not only to the women but to their party leaders.

Before the final vote to ratify began, suffragists were not sure how representatives Harry Burn and Banks Turner would vote. Burn had voted with the antis and Turner had voted with the suffragists on the motion to table the resolution.

Since only a simple majority was required, rather than a two-thirds vote, the suffragists needed just one more vote. With their hearts in their throats, they waited for the next roll call.

When his name was called, Burn voted yes, and the crowd broke into roars and applause. Twenty-four-year-old Burn, a legislator from an anti-suffragist district in the mountains, had listened to his mother, who had encouraged him to vote for ratification.[8]

Silence settled over the gallery again as the roll call approached Turner's name. One of the governor's closest friends, Turner had never stated that he was against ratification, but suffragists had not counted him among their ranks. When Turner answered yes in a "solemn, low voice," the crowd yelled and clapped, and stomped and cheered.[9] Some laughed one minute and cried the next.

Speaker of the House Seth Walker changed his vote from no to yes and introduced a motion to reconsider. He changed his vote because according to house rules, a move to reconsider could be made only by a representative on the winning side. The motion to reconsider was held up for days while the antis tried to get enough votes to defeat the measure on a second vote. But the pro-suffrage members did not budge.

On the morning of August 26, 1920, Secretary of State Bainbridge Colby issued a proclamation declaring that Tennessee had ratified and that the women's suffrage amendment was part of the Constitution of the United States.

When word reached Alice Paul that Tennessee had ratified, she sewed the thirty-sixth star on the ratification banner—the victory banner—and unfurled it over a second-story balcony for all to see.

One Hundred Years

Susan B. Anthony, the movement's greatest crusader, had died without seeing the fruit of her labor. Days before she died in 1906, she said to Anna Howard Shaw, "Just think of it, Anna, I have been striving for over sixty years for a little bit of justice no bigger than that, and yet I must die without obtaining it. Oh, it seems so cruel!"[10]

But Susan B. Anthony's decades of work were not in vain. One hundred years after Anthony's birth, 20 million women finally won the right to vote in the United States.

EPILOGUE

It took more than seventy years after the Seneca Falls Women's Rights Convention of 1848 for women to win the right to vote. In 1920, the Nineteenth Amendment, granting women suffrage, became law.

By the 1990s, seventy years after passage of the amendment, neither the fears of its critics nor the expectations of its supporters had become reality. The family did not collapse, nor did women's political involvement become equal to men's. Winning the right to vote, however, was the first step on the road toward equality between men and women.

Janet Reno became the first female United States attorney general and Madeleine Albright became the first female secretary of state in the 1990s. The number of women in Cabinet-level positions was 40.9 percent in 1997.[1]

But the number of women in Congress in 1997 was nowhere near equal to men: Only 47 of the 435 seats in the

House of Representatives were held by women, and of the one hundred Senate seats, only nine were held by women.[2]

Though laws were enacted to end discrimination against women in education—Title IX of the Civil Rights Act of 1972—it took until August 1997 for the last state-supported all-male school to admit women. That year, thirty female cadets were admitted to Virginia Military Institute, ending 158 years of male-only enrollment policy at that school.[3]

In economic matters, women still lagged behind men in the late 1990s, earning only 68 to 70 percent of men's pay.[4]

The pace of women's equality in politics, education, and economics has been slow but continual since the ratification of the Nineteenth Amendment in 1920. If the movement's first philosopher, Elizabeth Cady Stanton, were still alive today, she would undoubtedly be impatient with the progress, just as she was during her lifetime.

Susan B. Anthony, the movement's first general, would probably continue to repeat her last public words until total equality between men and women became a reality:

"Failure is impossible!"[5]

☆ TIMELINE ☆

1848—*July 19, 20*: First women's rights convention held in Seneca Falls, New York.

1850—*October 23*: The first National Women's Rights Convention is held in Worcester, Massachusetts.

1852—*April*: First meeting of Women's New York State Temperance Society.

1861—Civil War diverts suffragists' energies.

1866—*May 1*: Elizabeth Cady Stanton and Susan B. Anthony establish the American Equal Rights Association (AERA).

June: The Fourteenth Amendment is passed.

1868—Fourteenth Amendment ratified; The word *male* is used for the first time in the Constitution.

1869—The AERA splits over the word *male* in the Fourteenth Amendment and the exclusion of the word *sex* in the proposed Fifteenth Amendment; Lucy Stone forms the American Woman Suffrage Association (AWSA); The first bill supporting women's suffrage is introduced; Women win the right to vote in Wyoming Territory.

May: Anthony and Stanton form the National Woman Suffrage Association (NWSA).

1870—Fifteenth Amendment, which makes it clear that no state can deny the right to vote based on race, is passed.

1871—Women go to the polls to attempt to vote.

1875—Virginia Minor sues the registrar's office in St. Louis, Missouri, for denying her the right to vote; United States Supreme Court rules against her.

1878—The first joint resolution for women's suffrage is introduced in Congress.

1887—*January 25*: First vote on women's suffrage taken in the Senate and defeated 2–1.

1890—The NWSA and the AWSA merge, forming the National American Woman Suffrage Association (NAWSA); The group launches a state-by-state campaign in hopes of a national amendment; Wyoming is the first state with full suffrage for women.

1893—The State of Colorado adopts a constitutional amendment—the first time male voters approve women's suffrage.

1896—Idaho and Utah women win suffrage.

1907—Harriot Stanton Blatch organizes the Equality League of Self-Supporting Women.

1910—New York City hosts its first suffrage parade; Women in Washington State win suffrage.

1911—Women win the right to vote in California.

1912—Women win suffrage in Arizona, Kansas, and Oregon.

1913—Illinois becomes the first state to win presidential election suffrage for women by a legislative enactment; Alice Paul and Lucy Burns organize the Congressional Union (CU), to lobby for a national amendment.

1914—Women in Nevada and Montana win suffrage through state constitutional amendments.

March 19: A second vote on the national women's suffrage amendment is defeated on the floor of the Senate: 35 yeas, 34 nays.

1915—*January 12*: The House of Representatives takes its first vote on the national women's suffrage amendment; It is defeated—174 yeas, 204 nays. Forty thousand suffragists march in New York City—the largest parade in that city's history.

1917—*January 10*: Pickets are stationed in front of the White House.

March: Paul and the CU form the National Woman's Party.

November 14: Night of terror occurs.

November 27, 28: President Woodrow Wilson pardons suffragists jailed on the night of terror; They are released.

Women citizens in North Dakota, Nebraska, Rhode Island, and New York win presidential suffrage; Arkansas women win participation in primary elections; Ohio women lose the vote after wets petition for repeal.

1918—*January 10*: The House takes its second vote on women's suffrage: The amendment passes by exactly two thirds: 274 yeas, 136 nays.

October 1: The women's suffrage amendment defeated in the Senate for the third time.

Michigan, South Dakota, and Oklahoma adopt state constitutional amendments; Texas women secure voting rights in primary elections.

1919—*February 10*: The suffrage amendment is brought up for its fourth vote in the Senate and fails by one vote.

May 21: The suffrage amendment is successful in the House—304 yeas, 89 nays.

June 4: The women's suffrage amendment is finally passed by the Senate.

Women living in Indiana, Maine, Missouri, Iowa, Minnesota, Ohio, Wisconsin, and Tennessee secure presidential suffrage.

1920—Women in Kentucky win presidential suffrage.

August 18: Tennessee becomes the thirty-sixth state to ratify the Susan B. Anthony amendment.

August 26: The secretary of state proclaims the Nineteenth Amendment to the U.S. Constitution.

☆ CHAPTER NOTES ☆

Chapter 1. Call to Action

1. Abigail Adams, "We Are Determined to Foment a Rebellion," in Jerome Agel, ed., *Words That Make America Great* (New York: Random House, 1997), p.14.

2. Sherna Gluck, *From Parlor to Prison: Five American Suffragists Talk about Their Lives* (New York: Vintage Books, 1976), p. viii.

3. Kathleen Barry, *Susan B. Anthony: A Biography of a Singular Feminist* (New York: New York University Press, 1988), p. 23.

4. Ellen Carol DuBois, *The Elizabeth Cady Stanton–Susan B. Anthony Reader: Correspondence, Writings, Speeches*, rev. ed. (Boston: Northeastern University Press, 1992), p. 10.

5. Ibid., p. 14.

6. DuBois, p. 14.

7. Ibid., p. 15.

8. Barry, p. 18.

9. Ibid., p. 19.

10. Ibid., pp. 48, 50.

11. Ibid., p. 50.

12. Ibid., p. 63.

13. Oliver Jensen, *The Revolt of American Women: A Pictorial History of the Century of Change from Bloomers to Bikinis—From Feminism to Freud* (New York: Harcourt, Brace and Company, 1952), p. 44.

14. Barry, p. 64.

15. Ibid., pp. 64–65.

Chapter 2. A Nation at War

1. Marjorie Spruill Wheeler, *One Woman, One Vote: Rediscovering the Woman Suffrage Movement* (Troutdale, Ore.: NewSage Press, 1995), p. 18.

2. Aileen S. Kraditor, *The Ideas of the Woman Suffrage Movement, 1890–1920* (New York: Columbia University Press, 1965), p. 2.

3. Nancy F. Cott, *Root of Bitterness: Documents of the Social History of American Women* (New York: E. P. Dutton & Co., Inc., 1972), p. 14.

4. Wheeler, p. 56.

5. Ibid.

6. Ibid.

7. Ellen Carol DuBois, *The Elizabeth Cady Stanton–Susan B. Anthony Reader: Correspondence, Writings, Speeches*, rev. ed. (Boston: Northeastern University Press, 1992), p. 22.

8. Ibid.

9. Ibid.

10. Mari Jo Buhle and Paul Buhle, *The Concise History of Woman Suffrage* (Urbana, Ill.: University of Illinois Press, 1978), p. 15.

11. Ibid.

12. DuBois, p. 89.

13. Ibid., p. 91.

14. Buhle and Buhle, p. 17.

15. DuBois, p. 93.

16. Buhle and Buhle, pp. 19–20.

Chapter 3. One Woman Votes

1. Aileen S. Kraditor, *The Ideas of the Woman Suffrage Movement, 1890–1920* (New York: Columbia University Press, 1965), p. 111.

2. Ellen Carol DuBois, *The Elizabeth Cady Stanton–Susan B. Anthony Reader: Correspondence, Writings, Speeches*, rev. ed. (Boston: Northeastern University Press, 1992), p. 102.

3. Ibid., p. 103.

4. Ibid., p. 107.

5. Kathleen Barry, *Susan B. Anthony: A Biography of a Singular Feminist* (New York: New York University Press, 1988), pp. 249–250.

6. Ibid., p. 250.

7. Ibid.

8. Ibid., p. 251.

9. Ibid., p. 252.

10. Ibid.

11. Mari Jo Buhle and Paul Buhle, *The Concise History of Woman Suffrage* (Urbana, Ill.: University of Illinois Press, 1978), p. 295.

12. Ibid., p. 296.

13. DuBois, p. 107.

Chapter 4. Movement West

1. Marjorie Spruill Wheeler, *One Woman, One Vote: Rediscovering the Woman Suffrage Movement* (Troutdale, Ore.: NewSage Press, 1995), p. 291.

2. Mary Gray Peck, *Carrie Chapman Catt: A Biography* (New York: The H.W. Wilson Company, 1944), pp. 76–77.

Chapter 5. Some Rights Extended

1. Aileen S. Kraditor, *The Ideas of the Woman Suffrage Movement, 1890–1920* (New York: Columbia University Press, 1965), p. 62.

2. Sherna Gluck, *From Parlor to Prison: Five American Suffragists Talk about Their Lives* (New York: Vintage Books, 1976), p. 15.

3. Marjorie Spruill Wheeler, *One Woman, One Vote: Rediscovering the Woman Suffrage Movement* (Troutdale, Ore.: NewSage Press, 1995), p. 15.

4. Kraditor, p. 27.

5. Mari Jo Buhle and Paul Buhle, *The Concise History of Woman Suffrage* (Urbana, Ill.: University of Illinois Press, 1978), p. 22.

Chapter 6. African-American Suffragists

1. Kathleen Barry, *Susan B. Anthony: A Biography of a Singular Feminist* (New York: New York University Press, 1988), p. 173.

2. Marjorie Spruill Wheeler, *One Woman, One Vote: Rediscovering the Woman Suffrage Movement* (Troutdale, Ore.: NewSage Press, 1995), p. 13.

3. Ibid.

4. Howard Zinn, *A People's History of the United States* (New York: Harper & Row, Publishers, 1980), p. 122.

5. Ibid., p. 180.

6. Wheeler, p. 364.

7. Ibid., p. 147.

8. Ibid., p. 148.

Chapter 7. Fractured

1. Marjorie Spruill Wheeler, *One Woman, One Vote: Rediscovering the Woman Suffrage Movement* (Troutdale, Ore.: NewSage Press, 1995), pp. 57–58.

2. Ellen Carol DuBois, *The Elizabeth Cady Stanton–Susan B. Anthony Reader: Correspondence, Writings, Speeches*, rev. ed. (Boston: Northeastern University Press, 1992), p. 184.

3. Ibid., p. 186.

4. DuBois, p. 190.

5. Kathleen Barry, *Susan B. Anthony: A Biography of a Singular Feminist* (New York: New York University Press, 1988), p. 286.

6. Ibid., p. 340.

7. Sherna Gluck, *From Parlor to Prison: Five American Suffragists Talk about Their Lives* (New York: Vintage Books, 1976), p. 17.

8. Mary Gray Peck, *Carrie Chapman Catt: A Biography* (New York: The H. W. Wilson Company, 1944), pp. 174–175.

9. Gluck, p. 17.

10. Peck, p. 185.

Chapter 8. New Century, Old Battle

1. Kathleen Barry, *Susan B. Anthony: A Biography of a Singular Feminist* (New York: New York University Press, 1988), p. 355.

2. Ibid., p. 330.

3. Ibid., p. 290.

4. Ibid., p. 355.

5. Ibid., pp. 357–358.

6. Marjorie Spruill Wheeler, *One Woman, One Vote: Rediscovering the Woman Suffrage Movement* (Troutdale, Oreg.: NewSage Press, 1995), p. 12.

7. Mary Gray Peck, *Carrie Chapman Catt: A Biography* (New York: The H. W. Wilson Company, 1944), p. 281.

Chapter 9. New Tactics

1. Mary Gray Peck, *Carrie Chapman Catt: A Biography* (New York: The H. W. Wilson Company, 1944), pp. 230–231.

2. Inez Haynes Irwin, *The Story of the Woman's Party* (New York: Harcourt, Brace and Company, 1921), p. 7.

3. Ibid., p. 12.

4. Sherna Gluck, *From Parlor to Prison: Five American Suffragists Talk about Their Lives* (New York: Vintage Books, 1976), p. 19.

5. Marjorie Spruill Wheeler, *One Woman, One Vote: Rediscovering the Woman Suffrage Movement* (Troutdale, Ore.: NewSage Press, 1995), p. 306.

Chapter 10. Another War

1. Eleanor Flexner, *Century of Struggle: The Woman's Rights Movement in the United States*, rev. ed. (Cambridge, Mass.: The Belknap Press, 1975), p. 292.

2. Marjorie Spruill Wheeler, *One Woman, One Vote: Rediscovering the Woman Suffrage Movement* (Troutdale, Ore.: NewSage Press, 1995), p. 310.

3. Sherna Gluck, *From Parlor to Prison: Five American Suffragists Talk about Their Lives* (New York: Vintage Books, 1976), p. 237.

4. Wheeler, p. 288.

5. Ibid., p. 286.

6. Ibid., pp. 291–292.

7. Gluck, p. 22.

8. Wheeler, p. 292.

9. Ibid.

Chapter 11. Final Battle

1. Kathleen Barry, *Susan B. Anthony: A Biography of a Singular Feminist* (New York: New York University Press, 1988), p. 354.

2. Mari Jo Buhle and Paul Buhle, *The Concise History of Woman Suffrage* (Urbana, Ill.: University of Illinois Press, 1978), p. 307.

3. Mary Gray Peck, *Carrie Chapman Catt: A Biography* (New York: The H. W. Wilson Company, 1944), p. 297.

4. Ibid., p. 298.

5. Inez Haynes Irwin, *The Story of the Woman's Party* (New York: Harcourt, Brace and Company, 1921), p. 447.

6. Ibid., pp. 448–449.

7. Peck, p. 333.

8. Ibid., p. 335.

9. Irwin, p. 462.

10. Barry, p. 355.

Chapter 12. Epilogue

1. Ruth Gadebusch, "Suffrage for Women Has a Long Way to Go," *The Fresno Bee*, August 23, 1997, p. B7.

2. Ibid.

3. David Reed, "Virginia Military Institute Starts First Year with Women," *The Fresno Bee*, August 18, 1997, p. B3.

4. Carl Hartman, "Pay for Women Has Increased, But Not Enough, Says Report," *The Fresno Bee*, July 30, 1996, p. A6.

5. Kathleen Barry, *Susan B. Anthony: A Biography of a Singular Feminist* (New York: New York University Press, 1988), p. 354.

☆ FURTHER READING ☆

Bausum, Ann. *With Courage and Cloth: Winning the Fight for a Woman's Right to Vote*. Washington, D.C.: National Geographic Children's Books, 2004.

Bingham, Jane. *Women at War: The Progressive Era, World War I and Women's Suffrage, 1900–1920*. New York: Chelsea House Pub., 2011.

Frost, Elizabeth. *Women's Suffrage in America*. New York: Facts on File, 2005.

Landau, Elaine, *Women's Right to Vote*. New York: Scholastic Children's Press, 2005.

Rau, Dana Meachen. *Great Women of the Suffrage Movement*. Mankato MN: Compass Point Books, 2005.

☆ INDEX ☆